ANCIENT OF DAYS
Daniel 7:9, 13, 22

Anointed One
Psalm 2:2

(lined writing space)

Apostle
Hebrews 3:1

(lined writing space)

ARM OF THE LORD
Isaiah 53:1

AUTHOR OF ETERNAL SALVATION
Hebrews 5:9

Author of our Faith
Hebrews 12:2

Author of Peace
1 Corinthians 14:33

Avenger
1 Thessalonians 4:6

Beginning
Revelation 21:6

Bishop of Souls
1 Peter 2:25

Blessed and Holy Ruler
1 Timothy 6:15

BRANCh
Jeremiah 33:15, Isaiah 11:1

BREAD OF GOD
John 6:33

Bread of Life
John 6:35

Breath of Life
Genesis 2:7, Revelation 11:11

BRIDEGROOM
Isaiah 62:5, Matthew 9:15, 25:1-10

BRIGHT MORNING STAR
Revelation 22:16

BUCKLER
2 Samuel 22:31, Psalm 18:2, Psalm 18:30, Proverbs 2:7

CAPTAIN OF SALVATION
Hebrews 2:10

CARPENTER
Mark 6:3

CHIEF SHEPHERD
1 Peter 5:4

Chosen One
Isaiah 42:1

Christ
Matthew 1:16, 22:42

CHRIST OF GOD
Luke 9:20

CHRIST THE LORD
Luke 2:11

Christ, Son of the Living God
Matthew 16:16

Comforter
John 14:16, 26

COMMANDER
Isaiah 55:4

CONSOLATION OF ISRAEL
Luke 2:25

Consuming Fire
Deuteronomy 4:24, Hebrews 12:29

Cornerstone
Isaiah 28:16

COUNSELOR
Isaiah 9:6

CREATOR
1 Peter 4:19, Romans 1:25

CROWN OF BEAUTY

Isaiah 28:5

DAYSPRING

Luke 1:78

Deliverer

Romans 11:26; Psalm 18:2, 40:17, 70:5, 144:2

Desire of all Nations

Haggai 2:7

Diadem of Beauty
Isaiah 28:5

Door
John 10:7

DWELLING PLACE
Psalm 90:1

EAGLE
Deuteronomy 32:11, Exodus 19:4

ELECT ONE
Isaiah 42:1

EL CHAIYAI: The God of My Life
Psalm 42:8

EL-CHANNUM: The Gracious God
Jonah 4:2

EL DE'OT: The God of Knowledge
1 Samuel 2:3

EL ECHAD: The One God
Malachi 2:10

EL ELYON: God Most High
Genesis 14:20, Psalm 9:2

EL EMET: The God of Truth
Psalm 31:5

EL EREKH APAYIM AVI HA-TANCHUMIM:
God of Patience and Consolation
Romans 15:5, Isaiah 57:18

EL GIBBOR: The Mighty God
Isaiah 9:6

EL HAGGADOL: The Great God
Deuteronomy 10:17

El Hakkavod: The God of Glory
Psalm 29:3

El Hakkadosh: The Holy God
Isaiah 5:16

EL HANNE'EMAN: Faithful God

Deuteronomy 7:9

_____
_____
_____
_____
_____
_____
_____
_____
_____
_____
_____
_____

EL HANNORA: The Awesome God

Nehemiah 9:32

_____
_____
_____
_____
_____
_____
_____
_____
_____
_____
_____
_____

EL HASHAMAYIM: God of the Heavens
Psalm 136:26

EL-KANNO: The Jealous God
Exodus 20:5, 34:14, Numbers 5:14, 30

El malei Rachamim: God Full of Mercy
Psalm 59:10, 17, 66:20, 86:15

Elohim: God (plural)
Genesis 1:1, Isaiah 62:5

EL OLAM: Eternal God
Genesis 21:33, Psalm 90:1-3, 93:2, Isaiah 26:4

EL RACHUM: The God of Compassion
Deuteronomy 4:31

EL ROI: God Who Sees Me
Genesis 16:13

EL SALI: God of My Strength; God My Rock
Psalm 42:9

El Shaddai: All-Sufficient God, God Almighty

Genesis 17:1

El Tsaddik: The Righteous God

Isaiah 45:21

EL YESHUATI: God of My Salvation
Isaiah 12:2

EL YESUATENU: God Our Savior
Psalm 68:19

EL YESHURUN: God of Jeshurun ('The Righteous People')
Deuteronomy 32:15, 33:5, 26, Isaiah 44:2

EL YISRAEL: God of Israel
Psalm 68:36

Emmanuel
Matthew 1:23

End
Revelation 21:6

ETERNAL LIFE
1 John 5:20

ETERNAL SPIRIT
Hebrews 9:14

EVERLASTING FATHER
Isaiah 9:6

EVERLASTING GOD
Genesis 21:33

EXCELLENT
Psalm 148:13

Faithful
Revelation 19:11

Faithful Witness
Revelation 1:5

FATHER
Matthew 6:9

FATHER OF THE FATHERLESS
Psalm 68:5

Father of the Heavenly Lights
James 1:17

First
Isaiah 44:6, 48:12, Revelation 1:17, 2:8, 22:13

FIRSTBORN
Romans 8:29, Revelation 1:5, Colossians 1:15

FIRSTFRUITS
1 Corinthians 15:20-23

FORTRESS
Jeremiah 16:19, Psalm 18:2, 31:3, 71:3, 91:2, 144:2

FOUNDATION
1 Corinthians 3:11

FOUNTAIN OF LIVING WATERS

Jeremiah 2:13

FRIEND

Matthew 11:19

Fullers' (Launderers') Soap
Malachi 3:2

Gentle Whisper
1 Kings 19:12

GATE
John 10:7

GIFT OF GOD
John 4:10

Glory of the Lord
Isaiah 40:5

God
Genesis 1:1, Psalm 5:2, 7:1,

God Almighty
Genesis 17:1, Exodus 6:3

God of the Whole Earth
Isaiah 54:5

God Over All
Romans 9:5

God Who Sees Me
Genesis 16:13

GOODNESS
Psalm 144:2

GOOD SHEPHERD
John 10:11, 14

GOVERNOR
Psalm 22:28

GREAT HIGH PRIEST
Hebrews 4:14

Head of the Body

Colossians 1:18

Head of the Church

Ephesians 5:23

HEAVENLY FATHER
Matthew 6:26

HEIR OF ALL THINGS
Hebrews 1:2

Hiding Place
Psalm 32:7

Highest
Luke 1:76

High Priest

Hebrews 3:1, 4:14, 5:5-10

High Tower

Psalm 144:2

Holiness

1 Corinthians 1:30

Holy Ghost

John 14:26, Matthew 28:19, 1 John 5:7

Holy One
Acts 2:27

_____
_____
_____
_____
_____
_____
_____
_____
_____

Holy One of Israel
Isaiah 49:7

_____
_____
_____
_____
_____
_____
_____
_____
_____
_____
_____
_____

Holy Spirit
John 14:26, Luke 1:35

Hope
Titus 2:13

Horn of Salvation
Luke 1:69

Husband
Isaiah 54:5, Jeremiah 31:32, Hosea 2:16

I Am
Exodus 3:14, John 8:58

Image of God
2 Corinthians 4:4

IMAGE OF HIS PERSON
Hebrews 1:3

IMMANUEL
Isaiah 7:14

Intercessor
Romans 8:26-34, Hebrews 7:25

Jah
Psalm 68:4

Jealous
Exodus 34:14

Jehovah: The Lord
Psalm 83:18, Exodus 6:2-3

Jehovah-Adon Kal Ha'arets: Lord of Earth
Joshua 3:13

Jehovah-Bara: Lord Creator
Isaiah 40:28

Jehovah-Chatsahi: Lord My Strength
Psalm 27:1

Jehovah-Chereb: Glorious Sword
Deuteronomy 33:29

Jehovah-Eli: Lord My God
Psalm 18:2

Jehovah-Elyon: Lord Most High
Psalm 38:2

Jehovah-'Ez-Lami: Lord My Strength
Psalm 28:7

Jehovah-Gador Milchamah: Mighty in Battle
Psalm 24:8

JEHOVAH-GANAN: Lord Our Defense
Psalm 89:18

JEHOVAH-GO'EL: Lord My Redeemer
Isaiah 49:26, 60:16

Jehovah-Hamelech: Lord King
Psalm 98:6

Jehovah-Hashopet: Lord My Judge
Judges 11:27

Jehovah-Helech 'Olam: Lord King Forever
Psalm 10:16

Jehovah-Hoshe'ah: Lord Saves
Psalm 20:9

Jehovah-'Izoa Hakaboth: Lord Strong-Mighty

Psalm 24:8

Jehovah-'Immeku: Lord Is with You

Judges 6:12

Jehovah-Jireh: Lord Provider
Genesis 22:14, 1 John 4:9, Philippians 4:19

Jehovah-Kabodhi: Lord My Glory
Psalm 3:3

Jehovah-Kanna: Lord Jealous
Exodus 34:14

Jehovah-Keren-Yish'i: Horn of Salvation
Psalm 18:2

Jehovah-Machsi: Lord My Refuge
Psalm 91:9

_____
_____
_____
_____
_____
_____
_____
_____
_____
_____
_____
_____
_____
_____
_____

Jehovah-Magen: Lord My Shield
Deuteronomy 33:29

_____
_____
_____
_____
_____
_____
_____
_____
_____
_____
_____
_____
_____

Jehovah-Maken: Lord Who Strikes You
Ezekiel 7:9

Jehovah-Ma'ozi: Lord My Fortress
Jeremiah 16:19

Jehovah-Mekoddishkem:
Lord Who Makes You Holy
Exodus 31:13

_____
_____
_____
_____
_____
_____
_____
_____
_____
_____
_____
_____
_____
_____

Jehovah-Melech 'Olam: Lord King Forever
Psalm 10:16

_____
_____
_____
_____
_____
_____
_____
_____
_____
_____
_____
_____
_____
_____

Jehovah-Mephalti: Lord My Deliverer
Psalm 18:2

Jehovah-Metshodhathi: Lord My Fortress
Psalm 18:2

Jehovah-M'Gaddishcem: Lord My Sanctifier
Exodus 31:13

Jehovah-Misqabbi: Lord My High Tower
Psalm 18:2

Jehovah-M'Kaddesh: Sanctifier

1 Corinthians 1:30

Jehovah-Moshiech: Lord Your Savior

Isaiah 49:26, 60:16

Jehovah-Nissi: Lord My Banner
Exodus 17:15

Jehovah-Ori: Lord My Light
Psalm 27:1

Jehovah-Rohi: Lord My Shepherd
Psalm 23

Jehovah-Rophe: The Lord Who Heals You
Isaiah 53:4-5, Exodus 15:26

Jehovah-Sabaoth: Lord of Hosts
1 Samuel 1:3

Jehovah-Sel'i: Lord My Rock
Psalm 18:2

Jehovah-Shalom: Lord My Peace
Isaiah 9:6, Romans 8:31-35

Jehovah-Shammah: Lord Who Is Present
Hebrews 13:5

JEHOVAH-TSIDKENU: Lord Our Righteousness
1 Corinthians 1:30,

JEHOVAH-TSORI: Lord My Strength
Psalm 19:14

Jehovah-Uzam: Lord Strength in Trouble
Isaiah 49:26

Jehovah-Yasha: Lord My Savior
Isaiah 49:26

Jesus
Matthew 1:21, 25

Jesus Christ Our Lord
Romans 6:23

JUDGE
Isaiah 33:22, Acts 10:42

JUDGE OF THE WIDOWS
Psalm 68:5

Just One
Acts 22:14

Keeper
Psalm 121:5

KING
Zechariah 9:9, 14:16

KING ETERNAL
1 Timothy 1:17

King of Glory
Psalm 24:7-10

King of Jews
Matthew 27:11, John 19:19

KING OF KINGS
1 Timothy 6:15, Revelation 17:14

KING OF SAINTS
Revelation 15:3

LAMB

Revelation 5:6, 21:23, 22:3

LAMB OF GOD

John 1:29, 36

LAMB WHO WAS SLAIN FROM THE CREATION OF THE WORLD

Revelation 13:8

LAST

Isaiah 44:6, 48:12, Revelation 1:17, 2:8, 22:13

Last Adam
1 Corinthians 15:45

Lawgiver
Isaiah 33:22

LIGHT OF THE WORLD
John 8:12

EAGLE
Deuteronomy 32:11

LILY OF THE VALLEYS
Song 2:1

LION OF THE TRIBE OF JUDAH
Revelation 5:5

Living God
Daniel 6:20

Living Stone
1 Peter 2:4

LIVING WATER
John 4:10

LORD
John 13:13

Lord God Almighty
Revelation 15:3

Lord God of Hosts
Jeremiah 15:16

LORD JESUS CHRIST
1 Corinthians 15:57

LORD OF ALL
Acts 10:36

Lord of Glory
1 Corinthians 2:8

Lord of the Harvest
Matthew 9:38

LORD OF HOSTS
Haggai 1:5

LORD OF LORDS
1 Timothy 6:15

Lord Our Righteous Savior
Jeremiah 23:6

Love
1 John 4:8

LOVINGKINDNESS
Psalm 144:2

MAKER
Job 35:10, Psalm 95:6

Majesty on High
Hebrews 1:3

Man of Sorrows
Isaiah 53:3

Master
Luke 5:5

Mediator
1 Timothy 2:5

MERCIFUL GOD
Jeremiah 3:12

MESSENGER OF THE COVENANT
Malachi 3:1

MESSIAH
John 4:25

MIGHTY GOD
Isaiah 9:6

Mighty One
Isaiah 60:16

Mighty Warrior
Zephaniah 3:17, Jeremiah 20:11

Most Upright
Isaiah 26:7

Nazarene
Matthew 2:23

OFFSPRING OF DAVID
Revelation 22:16

OMEGA
Revelation 22:13

OUR PASSOVER LAMB
1 Corinthians 5:7

Our Peace
Ephesians 2:14

Overseer of Souls
1 Peter 2:25

Physician
Luke 4:23

Portion
Psalm 73:26, 119:57

POTENTATE
1 Timothy 6:15

POTTER
Isaiah 64:8

POWER OF GOD
1 Corinthians 1:24

PRINCE OF LIFE
Acts 3:15

Prince of Peace
Isaiah 9:6

Prophet
Acts 3:22

Propitiation
1 John 2:2, 4:10

PURIFIER
Malachi 3:3

QUICKENING SPIRIT
1 Corinthians 15:45

RABBONI: Teacher
John 20:16

RADIANCE OF GOD'S GLORY
Hebrews 1:3

Redeemer
Job 19:25

Redemption
1 Corinthians 1:30

REFINER'S FIRE
Malachi 3:2

REFUGE
Jeremiah 16:19

Resurrection
John 11:25

Rewarder
Hebrews 11:6

Righteousness
1 Corinthians 1:30

Righteous One
1 John 2:1

Rock
1 Corinthians 10:4

Root of David
Revelation 22:16

Root of Jesse
Isaiah 11:10

Rose of Sharon
Song of Songs 2:1

Ruler of God's Creation
Revelation 3:14

Ruler over Kings of Earth
Revelation 1:5

SAVIOR
Luke 2:11

Sceptre

Numbers 24:17

Seed

Genesis 3:15

SERVANT
Isaiah 42:1

SHADE
Psalm 121:5

Shepherd of our Souls
1 Peter 2:25

Shield
Genesis 15:1, 2 Samuel 22:31

SHILOH

Genesis 49:10

SONG

Exodus 15:2, Isaiah 12:2

Son of David

Matthew 1:1

Son of God

Matthew 27:54

SON OF MAN
Matthew 8:20

SON OF THE MOST HIGH
Luke 1:32

Source
Hebrews 5:9

Spirit
John 4:24

SPIRIT OF ADOPTION
Romans 8:15

SPIRIT OF COUNSEL
Isaiah 11:2

Spirit of Fear of the Lord
Isaiah 11:2

Spirit of God
Genesis 1:2

SPIRIT OF KNOWLEDGE
Isaiah 11:2

SPIRIT OF MIGHT
Isaiah 11:2

Spirit of the Lord
Hebrews 11:1

Spirit of Truth
John 14:17, 15:26, 16:13

SPIRIT OF UNDERSTANDING
Isaiah 11:2

SPIRIT OF WISDOM
Isaiah 11:2

STAR OUT OF JACOB
Numbers 24:17

STILL, SMALL VOICE
1 Kings 19:12

STRENGTH
Jeremiah 16:19

STONE
1 Peter 2:8

Stone of Israel
Genesis 49:24

Stronghold
Nahum 1:7

SUN OF RIGHTEOUSNESS

Malachi 4:2

Teacher
John 13:13

_____

_____

_____

_____

_____

_____

_____

_____

_____

_____

_____

_____

Temple
Revelation 21:22

_____

_____

_____

_____

_____

_____

_____

_____

_____

_____

_____

_____

The One
Psalm 144:2, 10

The One Who Is and Was and Is to Come
Revelation 11:17

True

Revelation 19:11

True Light

John 1:9

Vine
John 15:5

Wall of Fire
Zechariah 2:5

Wisdom of God
1 Corinthians 1:24, 30

WITNESS
Isaiah 55:4

WONDERFUL
Isaiah 9:6

WORD
John 1:1

WORD OF GOD
Revelation 19:13

Yah
Isaiah 12:2, Psalm 68:4

Yahweh: Lord, Jehovah
Genesis 2:4

Find your next journal at

More Than A Conqueror Books.com

Deep Bible studies, novels, and books for all ages that make a difference in the lives of those you care about.

Deepen your oneness with Christ through these Bible studies, journals, and other books from inspirational author

Mikaela Vincent

More Than A Conqueror Books.com

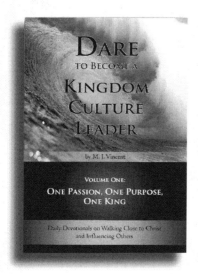 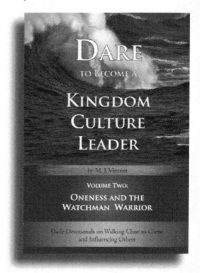

Dare to Become a Kingdom Culture Leader
Volume One: One Passion, One Purpose, One King
Volume Two: Oneness and the Watchman Warrior

Step into the destiny you were created for.
Become a Kingdom Culture Leader.

Whether you're a parent, teacher, pastor, missionary, worship leader, or even just Joe Blow Christian, this Bible study workbook to write in is for you. Through practical lessons on listening to God's voice, making wise decisions, following the Spirit's leading, walking in humility, promoting unity, and leading others well, author Mikaela Vincent uses small group Bible studies that can also be studied as a daily devotional to dig deep into the Bible and form new thought processes and habits so we can walk as one with Christ and lead out as Kingdom Culture influencers.
Dare to Become a Kingdom Culture Leader is based on the New Testament model of the church as the body of Christ, with the Lord as the Head, and offers steps for experiencing God, spiritual warfare, and following Jesus' calling in parenting, pastoring, mentoring and other leadership roles.

Dare to Be a Man of God

Powerful Bible studies for young men today on listening to God's voice and winning life's battles

Pull out your "sword" and get ready for a dive into the Word that just might change your life! This workbook for single men offers practical tools for knowing God's voice, overcoming strongholds, tapping into the Spirit's power, finding the wife your King has chosen for you, and pushing back the darkness.

Step into the adventure

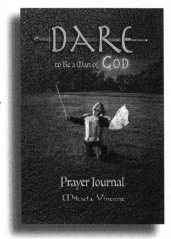

today, and dare to be a true man of God! A leader's guide is included, but the studies can also be done as private devotionals. We recommend this workbook for any single man 14 years and older. (For younger ages, try *Dare to Become a Man of God*).

Dare to Be a Man of God Prayer Journal

Take this companion to *Dare to Be a Man of God* into your quiet times for some exciting conversations with the King. Packed full with tools for recognizing God's voice and walking as one with Him, this notebook to write in is available with or without lines.

Dare to Become a Man of God

30 Bible studies from a mother's heart to her son's on drawing near to Christ and living victoriously.

Whether you like it or not, you are at war. Will you dare to defy enemy schemes? Will you dare to fight for the things that matter? Will you dare to become a man of God? Cartoons, personal stories, deep questions, practical how-to steps, and Scripture all point youth ages 12 and up to fix their eyes on Jesus and draw near to Him as they fight the good fight, listen to God's voice and make wise decisions through His guidance, so they can become more than conquerors through every tough situation life presents. A leader's guide is included, but this workbook can also be studied as a devotional in personal quiet times.

Delight to Be a Woman of God

Deep Bible studies for Christian single women today on listening to God's voice, walking in the Spirit, unlocking your beauty, and finding true love, happiness and freedom

Do you long for true love? Are you tired of falling into the same old messes again and again? Do you desire to be truly beautiful? Packed full with tools for hearing God's voice, finding freedom from strongholds and lies, and walking in the Spirit's power, this Bible study guide by Mikaela Vincent will strengthen your faith, transform your mind, and empower you

to overcome. A leader's guide is included, but this workbook can also be used for personal devotionals. Recommended for ages 14 and above. For younger women, try *Delight to Become a Woman of God*.

Delight to Be a Woman of God Prayer Journal

This companion to *Delight to Be a Woman of God* is full of tools for recognizing God's voice and walking as one with Him. Available with or without lines.

Delight to Become a Woman of God

30 Bible studies from a mother's heart to her daughter's on drawing near to Christ and loving well

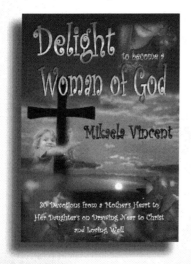

It's not a fairy tale. It's true. You really are a princess, destined to marry the King. And together you'll live happily forever after. It's all you ever dreamed life could be, and it's all yours, if you choose to become a woman of God. This Bible study guide for young women ages 12 and above, offers original illustrations, personal stories, deep questions, and Scripture to point young women to deeper depths with Christ so they can be set free from the things that keep them from the abundant life they were created for. A group study leader's guide is included. But this workbook can also be used for personal quiet times.

Fight evil and win. For real!

Dare to Be a Mighty Warrior

by Mikaela Vincent

100 Practical, effective spiritual warfare strategies for today's husband, father, single man of God. Find freedom from strongholds, protect the ones you love, listen to God's voice, live in His power, and win victory over darkness in the battlefield of the mind. Includes a checklist for sins and thought processes that lead us astray.

Dare to Be a Mighty Warrior Prayer Journal

Guided conversations with God for freedom from strongholds, wrong thought processes, and more. Accompanies the *Dare to Be a Mighty Warrior* spiritual warfare manual above, but with room to write and process your experiences as you walk out in the warfare strategies through daily life and experiences.

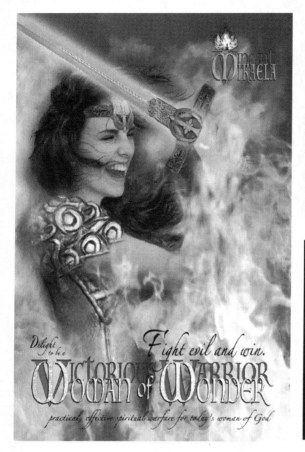

Delight to Be a Woman of Wonder
(Same practical, effective warfare tactics as *Dare to Be a Mighty Warrior*, but written for today's woman of God)

Delight to Be a Woman of Wonder Power Planner
(Day planner, calendar, agenda, goal organizer for handing every moment to the Lord, listening to His voice, and letting Him be her Time Manager, so she doesn't burn out)

Delight to Be a Woman of Wonder Prayer Journal
(Guided conversations with God that lead to freedom, power, and

www.MoreThanAConquerorBooks.com
(All proceeds the author receives go to sharing the Light in dark areas of the world where few have ever heard of Christ.)

Pure-As-Gold Children's Books
by Mikaela Vincent
www.MoreThanAConquerorBooks.com
Equipping young hearts today
for the battles of tomorrow.

Out You Go, Fear!

Is your child afraid of the night? Does he sometimes "see" monsters in the dark? Does she have nightmares or awake in a panic? Do you? This story about a fearful, but eventually brave boy addresses night fears most children experience. Through colorful pictures, sound truths, and a fun storyline, Vincent offers children ages 4-8 (and parents too!) steps to freedom from fear so they can sleep in peace. Includes tips for parents on helping their children to freedom from nightmares and the effects of traumatic memories.

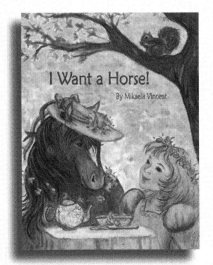

I Want a Horse

Have you ever wanted something so much it was all you could think of or dream about? In this inspirational picture book for ages 4-8, Mikaela Vincent uses colorful artwork, imaginative poetry and heartwarming humor to tell the story of a young girl who asks for her heart's desire only to discover a treasure she already has that surpasses her imaginations. Moms and daughters will especially enjoy a deep bond reading together this fun interchange between an ambitious little girl and her wise and creative mother.

I Want to See Jesus

This easy-to-read book for ages 3-7 uses colorful drawings and simple words to teach just-beginning readers that Jesus is always with us, even when we can't see Him.

Chronicles of the Kingdom of Light
fantasy with deep, life-transforming purpose
by Mikaela Vince

Based on stories created by Mikaela Vincent to help her children live who they are in Christ, some have compared these first two books in the *Chronicles of the Kingdom of Light* to the *Chronicles of Narnia* because of the inspirational allegory filled with adventure, humor, illustrations, and truths that just might change your life, including freedom from fear, lies, and strongholds.

Book 1: Rescue from Darkness

Snatched from their summer fun by a sudden tragedy, six friends loyal to the King of Light embark upon an unforgettable adventure into the Kingdom of Darkness to rescue a young boy held hostage by evil creatures.

Astride such mystical mounts as a winged tiger, a flying unicorn, and a giant cobra, these ordinary young people engage in an extraordinary battle that will cost them more than they counted on. As they struggle against monsters — and even each other — to overcome the fight against night, the friends soon discover the true enemy that must be conquered is the enemy within themselves.

Book 2: Sands of Surrender

Banished by the King of Light, Cory cannot continue the search for his kidnapped brother until he discovers a way back into the Kingdom of Darkness where the boy is held prisoner.

When creatures of Darkness offer to lead him there, his decision to follow costs him his freedom and exposes a plot against his family so dangerous he may not make it out alive.

Meanwhile, Victoria sets out on her own misadventure to rescue her friend, but her decisions place those she loves in such terrible peril, Cory's life is not the only one she must save.

More Journals by Mikaela Vincent
notebooks to write in for all ages
8.5x11 or 6x9 inches
Available blank, with lines, or bullet (dot matrix) from
www.MoreThanAConquerorBooks.com

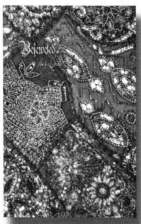

Names of God
Prayer Journal

Bejeweled: Touch
of India Journal

Soar on Eagle
Wings Journal

Finding Beauty
among the Ruins
Adventure Journal

Horse Lovers
Journal

Friesian Horse
Lovers Journal

*We're not just about books. We're about books that make a
difference in the lives of those you care about.*

Made in the USA
Middletown, DE
03 November 2020